SHAWN HENDERSON

INTERIORS IN CONTEXT

Mayer Rus

Photographs by Stephen Kent Johnson

CONTENTS

7   Introduction
     Mayer Rus

13   My West Village Apartment

25   Aspen Modern Retreat

45   Greenwich Village Town House

65   West Village Residence

77   Montana Chalet

99   River-View Apartment

113   Connecticut Farmhouse

129   High Line Apartment

139   Hamptons Waterfront Retreat

153   My Hillsdale Home

171   Aspen Ranch

183   French Quarter Town House

199   Utah Mountain House

217   Mississippi Country Estate

237   Acknowledgments

238   Credits

INTRODUCTION

In an arena as rarefied as high-end interior design, where affectation and fabulousness often run amok, Shawn Henderson's work makes a compelling case for the power of quiet, confident grace. He has a gift for crafting spaces that feel intuitive, easy, almost inevitable. At the same time, he conjures environments of extraordinary sophistication and beauty, environments that belie the painstaking effort of their creation, as if the designer's role was somehow incidental. His interiors are comfort perfected, everyday life ennobled. They are invitations to sit back and renew, or simply to look at oneself anew.

Surveying the body of his work—from majestic mountain homes and country cottages to sophisticated urban aeries and town houses—a readily apparent Henderson signature is difficult to discern. His approach eschews instantly identifiable decorative gestures meant to signify authorship. Henderson's ego is subsumed in his mission to craft environments exquisitely tailored to the specific needs and spirit of the people he serves. Certain homes present a decidedly traditional face, while others adhere more closely to the tenets of classic modernism. Most of his projects, in fact, plumb the tension between the traditional and the modern, blurring the boundaries between those increasingly antiquated distinctions.

The great American decorator Billy Baldwin famously quipped, "If you can tell I did a house, I didn't. The essence of the relationship between client and decorator must be *we*." The same is true for Henderson. Each project he creates is unique, fondly and attentively detailed to channel the desires of his clients, a product of *we*. And yet, no matter the register, there are subtle threads running through his work, detectable to anyone who shares Henderson's vision of unpretentious luxury. His work evinces a clarity of line and purpose that allows the two halves of "lifestyle" to resonate independently and, even more profoundly, together. That clarity comes to life in the multimodal, look-and-touch invitation of every curve and texture and finish in the rooms he orchestrates.

The essence of Henderson's sensibility and aesthetic can perhaps be summed up in one simple imperative—hospitality. Growing up as one of six children with parents who ran a popular tavern, hospitality and the creation of welcoming environments are keynotes in the designer's life and work. Beneath broad hallmarks like orderliness and serenity and comfort, beneath the subtly distinguished spaces and inviting kitchens and bespoke details by the thousands, his interiors possess the generosity, compassion, and consideration of an accomplished host. These are places designed to welcome friends and family, and every arrival feels unquestionably like a homecoming.

It's telling that the wingback chair is the most ubiquitous piece of furniture in all of Henderson's far-flung interiors, appearing in one form or another in nearly every project illustrated in this volume. The venerable wingback came into popularity as the British were colonizing America, and it caught on in the new territories as a form of climate control, to hold warmth and protect sitters from drafts. The chair feels like a succinct representation of Henderson's approach to interior design, being both private and public—you can hide in it, or not, simply by shifting posture. It's equally telling that Henderson's favorite interpretation of the wingback is Danish design maestro Hans Wegner's beloved Papa Bear chair. Wegner's design precisely encapsulates multiple points of cultural contact—an Anglo-American form updated through a Scandinavian lens, preserving the best of the original but reimagined for modern life. In essence, this is the core of Henderson's design credo: hold warmth, protect the inhabitants, nurture tranquility, embrace modernity.

Chairs are arguably the most contemplative and intimate piece of furniture in the designer's arsenal. As Wegner stated, "The chair is the closest thing to people, which is why it is important to take perfect care of every detail. I feel the details as much as I can see them. People touch the piece, they see with their hands." Like the synesthetic collapse between sight and touch that Wegner evokes, Henderson's work is always guided by both the visual and the textural. In a broader sense, his spaces are distinctly sculptural, crafted to be appreciated from all sides. They are attuned to the rhythms and rituals of contemporary life, not the flattening gaze of the camera. This conception of design—shaping space as opposed to merely filling it—finds a nice echo in the Danish word for design, *formgivning*, which literally means "giving shape." That definition, that idea, positions Henderson as a curator of space as much as objects.

Wegner is hardly alone in the designer's pantheon of great Danes. Henderson's interiors are chockablock with signature creations by the likes of Frits Henningsen, Kaare Klint, Ole Wanscher, Arne Jacobsen, Finn Juhl, and other legends of Scandinavian modernism. In the annals of design history, those pioneering talents are justifiably renowned for their artistry in reinterpreting historical forms in midcentury vernacular, using traditional techniques and an elevated appreciation for materials to imbue the spare lines of modernism with a startlingly new sense of richness and elegance. This time-shifting alchemy is perfectly in sync with Henderson's values of unaffected beauty and honesty of material and line. Like the visible joinery of a Danish modern chair, Henderson imbues his interiors with a deeply felt solidness and dependability. There is nothing extra or tricky; everything is just what it seems to be, what it needs to be, to do its job.

Of course, this plain, commonsense honesty is also a hallmark of classic Americana, and Henderson's interiors are nothing if not American in their lack of pretension, polyglot brio, and forward-looking optimism. Unconcerned with faddishness or trends, the designer teases beauty only from that which feels appropriate, seemly, relevant. His rooms place a premium on democratic appreciation rather than elitist connoisseurship. Even in homes that boast a king's ransom in masterworks of design, Henderson's unfussy ensembles of pedigreed treasures, custom pieces, and humble, unheralded vintage furnishings radiate a sense of affability and confidence, much like the man himself.

The British textile maven and polymath William Morris summarized the purview of the interior designer as a straightforward proposition: "To give people pleasure in the things they must perforce use, that is one great office of decoration," he averred. That sentiment underscores both the utilitarian responsibility and the lofty ambitions of the decorator's art. In Henderson's work, the quotidian realities of the homeowners' lives frame the parameters in which he conjures pleasure. His aesthetic virtuosity evolves organically from the exigencies of site and context and client—something thoughtfully composed rather than artificially imposed.

To comprehend a designer's true passions and priorities, one need only examine the nests they have feathered for themselves. And so it is with Henderson. His Manhattan apartment and his country house in upstate New York, both represented in this book, paint a revealing portrait of the designer, explicated in three dimensions. The soul of his compact Gotham lair emerges from the humble character, timeworn texture, and rich patina of the original nineteenth-century architecture, which he liberated from a straitjacket of wallpaper, paint, and aspirational moldings that had accrued over decades of renovation. Reclaimed wood beams, original pine floors, and rugged exposed brick now set the stage for an intensely personal, idiosyncratic drama.

The apartment's decor bears all the stylemarks of a quintessential Henderson interior. Vintage pieces from Denmark, Sweden, Italy, and England mingle amicably with comely American furnishings, all united by their distilled forms, understated lines, and assiduous avoidance of unnecessary ornament. Acknowledged all-stars of design history rub shoulders with unheralded and anonymous makers, sparking conversations both pithy and profound. Against this resonant backdrop, Henderson, in characteristic fashion, leaves plenty of room for delight—in a Victorian birdcage converted into a bar; in a vintage chalkboard repurposed as an artist's canvas; and in a contemporary weaving by Dougall Paulson that connects the century that was with the century that is.

At Henderson's country getaway in Hillsdale, old meets new, the rustic meets the refined, and the gulf between nature and human nature is elided. The designer's additions, renovations, and decorative ministrations all defer to the original nineteenth-century Eyebrow Colonial architecture, leveraging the charm of the past in the service of enhancing the present. Henderson's respect for the kinship between the natural and built environments comes to the fore in his strategic framing of views and landscape, his choice of companionable natural materials, and his finely calibrated color palette. His decorative juxtapositions once again accentuate the American/Scandinavian interface that Henderson has reiterated so poignantly in an endless variety of settings.

Naturally, every decision Henderson made is gauged to augment the pleasure and comfort of his guests. The siren call of serenity and joy emanates from the welcoming communal kitchen to the pale, blissful tones that bathe the bedrooms to, yes, the cozy wingback chair tucked in the living room. But the magic of Henderson's country refuge transcends colors and cabinetry, fabrics and finishes. When guests depart his home, the designer wants them to remember the mood and the experience, not how chic the Kaare Klint settee looks beside the fireplace.

That generosity of vision finds expression in the intangible qualities that animate all of Shawn Henderson's work, the qualities that make a house a home. In our image-driven culture of social media and instant gratification, his interiors act like a welcome tonic, reminding us that life is meant to be savored through all our senses, mind and body. What definition of luxury could be more profound?

MAYER RUS

MY WEST VILLAGE APARTMENT

A walk-up apartment in a modest tenement building was not exactly what I had in mind when I was searching for a new home in New York City. When my broker took me to see the space, I looked up at the unimpressive late nineteenth-century building and had no interest, despite its location on a block that was one of the quietest, quaintest, and most redolent of Old New York charm in the West Village. But once inside, I discovered an apartment with exposures on three sides, flooding the interior with natural light. I fell in love, made an offer, and got to work.

My first order of business was to strip away the remnants of decades of renovations—layers of wallpaper, elaborate moldings, and so on—that obscured the timeworn texture of the original architecture. I also removed several interior walls to create a loftlike layout more attuned to the way I live, with an open sweep of living, dining, and kitchen spaces, and added a powder room and walk-in closet. Reclaimed wood beams, minimal baseboard and door casing details, strategic pockets of exposed brick, and refinished pine floors from 1875 underscore the apartment's cozy, unpretentious ambience.

The furnishings scheme pairs favorite midcentury designs by Danish masters Hans Wegner, Frits Henningsen, Kaare Klint, and Ole Wanscher with decorative curiosities such as a floor-standing Victorian birdcage that I retrofitted as a bar, and art that I've acquired over many years. In the living room, I placed a Dunbar sofa—the most comfortable I've ever sat on—below a vintage chalkboard repurposed as a canvas for a commission by artist Gregory Siff. I love a quilted fabric and a bit of granny chic in an otherwise masculine space, so a pink chintz-upholstered armchair and ottoman were natural additions to the opposite corner—and an inviting place to sit with a coffee and the Sunday *Times*.

For a bit of textural diversity, I lined the walls of the petite powder room in cork and installed unlacquered brass fixtures for a note of contrast. The end result feels warm, soulful, discreetly dapper, and above all comfortable—my very personal retreat from the always exciting but often intense activity of New York City.

LESLIE WILLIAMSON

PAGE 12   In my dining room, I placed a set of Ole Wanscher chairs and a Kaare Klint sofa around a Hans Wegner table. The Scandinavian theme is amplified by a midcentury Swedish hanging light and Gunnar Nylund ceramic lamps. The rosewood folding screen is vintage and the art is a handwoven work by Dougall Paulson.

PAGE 15   My predilection for a touch of granny chic comes through in a lounge chair and ottoman covered in quilted pink chintz. The photographs hanging above are by Johnny Savage.

PAGES 16–17   I paired a vintage Dunbar sofa with Frits Henningsen wingback chairs and a 1950s Brazilian rosewood cocktail table in the living room. A vintage chalkboard was repurposed for a custom commission by artist Gregory Siff.

PAGE 19   Painted brick walls and original nineteenth-century pine floors help maintain the apartment's humble, historic character.

PAGE 20   Cork wall covering gives a small powder room its own sense of place.

PAGE 21   A Sam Still drawing surmounts a crisply tailored headboard in my bedroom, which features Kaare Klint sconces, Jacques Adnet end tables, and a sculpture by Will Gianotti on a plaster pedestal.

PAGE 22   A collection of furnishings, centered on an Ole Wanscher cabinet, demonstrates my commitment to a neutral palette animated by a variety of textures and finishes. The photograph is by Chris McCaw.

When I joined this project, the architecture of this Aspen house was already done—and done beautifully—by Studio B, under the direction of its founder, Scott Lindenau. The crisply tailored structure has a low horizontal profile that nestles into the landscape and rooms that open onto spectacular vistas of the surrounding mountains. My role was to bring a sense of cohesion and clarity to the interiors, consolidating the clients' estimable collection of art and furniture with pieces of my own design and important new additions.

While the overall mood is one of subdued sophistication—the setting itself provides splendor aplenty—I wanted to give the individual rooms their own sense of drama. The living room is the first space you encounter after climbing the stairs from the entry hall to the main floor. Spanning two sides of this large room, floor-to-ceiling windows offer awe-inspiring panoramas across the wooded valley to the snow-capped peaks of the Elk Mountains. Against this backdrop, I didn't want the room to feel overly decorated or cluttered, so I decided to go with big gestures: in the main living area, a brilliant, icy-blue Sam Orlando Miller faceted mirror, a curvaceous sheepskin-upholstered armchair by Danish architect Flemming Lassen, a cocktail table seven feet in diameter, and generously scaled seating pieces by my studio; and in a second seating space, a pair of Hans Wegner Papa Bear chairs. An enormous custom carpet designed to look like rugs layered over one another helps define more intimate areas within the voluminous expanse.

In the dining room, beneath a commanding multipaneled work by Tacita Dean, graceful Italian chairs from the 1950s surround a table by the contemporary French designer Martin Szekely, under a mobile-like lighting fixture by David Weeks. In the primary bedroom, a handsome platform bed by Studio B and a vintage Illum Wikkelso lounge chair defer to the breathtaking views. A striking Alexander Calder tapestry animates a comfortable rec room. Working in tandem with the clients' art collection— which includes large-scale works by Theaster Gates and Claudy Jongstra as well as by Dean and Calder—the decor provides a mellow backdrop to absorb the majesty of nature.

Spanish Colonial Style

The World of Khubilai Khan

PAGE 24 A Sam Orlando Miller faceted mirror commands the living room. The sheepskin-covered lounge chair is by Flemming Lassen.

PAGES 26–27 In the entry, an Antony Gormley sculpture is flanked by a Warren Platner stool and a custom concrete and blackened bronze bench by Eric Slayton. The tapestry hanging in the stairwell is by Claudy Jongstra.

PAGE 31 An artwork by Theaster Gates composed from decommissioned fire hoses holds a corner of the living room, where a Philip and Kelvin LaVerne bronze table nestles into the curve of a Vladimir Kagan sofa.

PAGES 34–35 A 1970s table by Stephen Surfs separates discrete seating areas. The Hans Wegner Papa Bear chairs find their way into many of my projects.

PAGE 36 A Brent Wadden woven painting adds color and movement to the primary bedroom.

PAGE 37 A custom cypress-wood Japanese soaking tub is cradled in a limestone niche in the primary bath.

PAGES 40–41 In the dining room, vintage 1950s Italian chairs surround a Martin Szekely table beneath a David Weeks chandelier. Tacita Dean's eight-part photogravure adds another landscape vista to a house with many views.

GREENWICH VILLAGE TOWN HOUSE

The renovation of this classic Greenwich Village town house was a delicate balancing act—weighing the push of historical preservation against the pull of contemporary inspiration. The structure was built in 1915 as a single-family residence and then converted into a multifamily dwelling; when my clients purchased the house, it was divided into ten apartments. Peter Pennoyer Architects, our partner in the transformation process, was tasked with restoring the house to its original purpose as a single-family home, replete with traditional moldings and paneling, fluted columns on the parlor floor, and a stunning central staircase. Our goal for both the architecture and the interiors was to pay homage to the house's period roots without capitulating to a dry, orthodox exercise in historical literalism. The renovation was not only a labor of love but also a setting for it: my clients were married at the construction site.

The polyglot language of the reconceived interiors is announced immediately in the entryway, where we combined a John Dickinson console with large-scale foliate Danish sconces from the 1940s, a midcentury French chandelier, and a painting by George Condo. The continental sensibility expands into the main social spaces on the parlor floor. In the living room, we tempered the formality of the architectural backdrop with sofas covered in an alluring Klein-blue velvet, and custom seating with poured-glass legs, an impressive seven-foot-long vintage Arredoluce chandelier, and a carpet and fire screen with a matching pattern drawn from an antique table. In the dining room, a sculptural Silas Seandel metal dining table with Paul Evans chairs is positioned off-center, juxtaposed with a custom corner banquette that has become a favorite lounging spot for the homeowners and their friends.

On the upper floors, variations in color, texture, and materials conspire to give the individual rooms their own distinct identities. The walls of the third-floor library are painted with a faux-bois treatment in a pale gray driftwood tone. The media room on the same level is sheathed in mauve velvet for a cozy, cloistering effect. In the moody primary bedroom, we covered the walls and bed frame in a purplish-gray felt, which we also used for the curtains. Throughout the house, decorative flourishes both playful and glamorous, and a continuously evolving art collection, leaven the seriousness of the architecture, conjuring an environment anchored in the past but animated by an exuberant contemporary spirit.

PAGE 44   The entry composition includes a John Dickinson console, a French midcentury chandelier, fanciful Danish sconces, and a George Condo painting.

PAGES 46–47   Artworks by Genieve Figgis, Fred Wilson, and Robert LaHotan adorn the living room. The furnishings ensemble encompasses a vintage Italian wingback chair, a custom sofa, an Angelo Lelli chandelier, and an Ico Parisi polyhedron-form bar.

PAGES 48–49   Seating options in the dining room include Paul Evans chairs around a Silas Seandel table and a custom corner banquette for informal lounging. Artworks by Tom Keyes and Mark Titchner hang by the fireplace.

PAGE 50   In the parlor stair hall, a Cindy Sherman photograph is joined by a Jansen-style sofa and slipper chair. The chandelier is by Bec Brittain.

PAGE 51   A Rebecca Warren sculpture is installed at the base of the stair.

PAGE 54   In the media room, a Wolfgang Tillmans photograph hangs against a mauve velvet wall covering.

PAGE 55   A Richard Prince painting joins a custom desk in the library.

PAGES 56–57   The library art installation includes photographs by Robert Mapplethorpe and Nan Goldin.

PAGES 58–59   The walls and bed frame in the moody primary bedroom are covered in a purplish-gray felt. The lounge chair and ottoman are by Lloyd Wright, and the artworks include photographs by Peter Hujar and Matthew Barney as well as a Tom Keyes painting above the fireplace.

PAGE 62   A Nathan Mabry sculpture commands the garden.

WEST VILLAGE RESIDENCE

For all its promise of generous, wide-open space, the idea of loft living—or loftlike living—has its drawbacks. When my clients acquired a Manhattan apartment in a Herzog & de Meuron–designed building on the Hudson River, I was challenged to reimagine the home's voluminous social area. Having worked with these clients before, I knew the way they lived, and I wanted to carve out a series of discrete spaces without compromising the airiness, light, and views. To this end, I designed a continuous ribbon of whitewashed cypress that delineates rooms and obscures service elements, an elegant and highly functional solution.

That project began at the front door, where I created a new entry hall that establishes a sense of arrival and decompression before one moves into the main living area, where the glorious river views unfold. Clad in the pale cypress, the minimalist entry opens into the apartment through a graceful archway that nods to the building's rounded forms.

Evening visitors are greeted with a kaleidoscope of colors ricocheting across the ceiling and walls, courtesy of *The Tetrahedral Night*, a light sculpture by Olafur Eliasson. The piece crowns an intimate setting of vintage Milo Baughman chairs clustered around a circular cocktail table. The cypress wall continues into the living room proper, which includes a seating area defined by grooved millwork around the fireplace, bathed in serene neutrals, with occasional wine-red accents to enliven the mix. The textural variety of the fabrics and other materials adds a richness and warmth to the crisp modern architecture. Muted, quiet tones extend into the primary bedroom, but in the children's rooms, the palette adds bright blues and greens.

One of the most crucial aspects of the assignment was establishing a separation between the living and dining areas, which I accomplished with a freestanding, semicircular divider in the same cypress that doubles as a small buffet. Like my other architectural interventions, the divider helps create different experiences from one space to the next. A panel concealed in the wall just to the right of the fireplace swings to meet the divider, enclosing the dining room. It was a true feat of engineering to make these architectural interventions connected and cohesive.

Throughout the home, one of my more contemporary spaces, artworks by Georg Baselitz, Tal R, Robert Longo, Leon Polk Smith, Leelee Kimmel, and others contribute to the ambience of calm, collected cool.

PAGE 64   A sculpture by Tal R and a Leon Polk Smith print inhabit the arched entry hall of
             pale cypress.

PAGE 66   An Olafur Eliasson light sculpture crowns a suite of vintage Milo Baughman lounge
             chairs just off the entry.

PAGE 67   Marcel Gascoin chairs pull up to an Angelo Mangiarotti table in the dining room.
             The painting is by Retna.

PAGES 68–69 Vintage standing lamps by Lisa Johansson-Pape are paired with A.J. Iversen
             armchairs in the living room.

PAGES 70–71 A vivid Rachel Howard painting provides a dramatic contrast to the purposefully
             monochromatic, understated palette of the living room.

PAGE 72   In a corner of the primary bedroom, a Beth Campbell branching mobile sculpture
             hangs above a vintage Edward Wormley sofa.

PAGE 74   A Robert Longo charcoal drawing graces a child's bedroom.

MONTANA CHALET

The mountainside location of this newly built ski-in/ski-out house at the Yellowstone Club in Big Sky, Montana, is undeniable and spectacular: driving to the site, I passed a moose with legs taller than my car and bighorn sheep hanging out on impossibly steep cliffs. For my clients, a family with three small children, I wanted to create a twenty-first-century interpretation of a traditional ski chalet—a place that honors the virtues of comfort and warmth while still radiating a vivid contemporary spirit suitable for a young family. That meant striking a balance between the rustic and the modern, the rough and the refined.

The interiors amplify the robust architectural scheme by Pearson Design Group while softening the house's muscular edges and rugged materials. Fieldstone and soft carpet, blackened steel and gingham fabric, reclaimed wood and plush shearling—they all live side by side, each the happier for the other. The overall look is meant to be considered but casual. There are certainly pedigreed pieces throughout—including a rare Hans Wegner chaise longue in the owners' bedroom and a set of pitch-perfect Robert "Mouseman" Thompson chairs in the breakfast nook—but nothing reads as pretentious or fussy. This is a home that fosters serenity, humble beauty, and repose, from the hearth of the four-sided fireplace in the après-ski room to the pared-down luxury of the bedrooms. This is also a home that regularly hosts gangs of family and friends of all ages, and it has the entertaining spaces, guest rooms, and bunk beds to prove it.

In keeping with the overall mood of relaxation, the color palette leans heavily on neutral tones that pay tribute to the architectural materials. Strategic shots of blue, orange, and peach enliven the subdued compositions, while varied textures in fabrics and wood grains add depth to the rooms. Ultimately, the interiors defer to the dazzling scenery that surrounds the house, which no amount of decorative bravado can hope to surpass.

PAGE 76   A 1970s Olavi Hänninen table echoes the rustic mood of the wood paneling in the entry. A chandelier by Lou Blass and a Warren Platner ottoman add contrast notes of cool metal.

PAGES 78–79   The furnishings ensemble in the living room encompasses pieces from the nineteenth, twentieth, and twenty-first centuries, buoying the atmosphere of timeless mountain chic.

PAGE 80   The pairing of a vintage gingham-covered wingback chair with a Roberto Giulio Rida sconce underscores the seamless integration of the traditional and the modern.

PAGE 83   In the breakfast nook, a sculptural lighting fixture by Doug Johnston nods to the forms of the mountain landscape. The chairs are by the British designer Robert "Mouseman" Thompson.

PAGES 84–85   A focal four-sided fireplace makes a perfect gathering spot for the serene après-ski room.

PAGES 86–87   The assiduously tranquil color palette of the primary bedroom emphasizes the space's function as a place of repose for mind and body.

PAGES 88–89   A classic Hans Wegner chaise longue holds a corner of the primary bedroom.

PAGE 93   A custom bunk bed picks up the architectural vocabulary of the room's white-painted wood beams.

PAGES 94–95   A Matthew Brandt photograph graces the ski room, where a custom sofa adds a strategic jolt of color.

RIVER-VIEW APARTMENT

For this pied-à-terre in New York City's West Village, I had the luxury of working with one of the chicest couples on the planet. They came to the table with a cultivated sense of personal style, sophisticated taste, and an eagerness to create something truly special. As any decorator will attest, this is the type of client who challenges you to do your most imaginative work.

My job here was to bring clarity, cohesion, and a bit of inspiration to the couple's vision. The space offered generously scaled rooms and exceptional views of the cityscape and Hudson River, but would take some effort to achieve the character that the wife, a gallerist, wanted: the feel of a lofty, Hausmannian Paris apartment, with compelling combinations of vintage furnishings and art from different periods. My layering process began with an establishing vignette in the entry that pairs a sinuous Gio Ponti mirror with an equally curvaceous Wendell Castle cloud-form shelf. To create a more intimate scale in the voluminous living room, I used individual carpets to loosely define two discrete seating areas. In the slightly more formal space, I placed a pair of Milo Baughman swivel chairs, upholstered in custom woven textiles by Toyine Sellers, next to Jacques Quinet cocktail tables, and a shapely Edward Wormley Party Sofa, so called because its sprung arms make a perfect spot to perch, martini in hand, during a get-together. The bespoke carpet below picks up the mustardy tone of the sofa's striking velvet upholstery. In the more casual space, a low, loungy Harvey Probber sectional faces a television cabinet covered in straw marquetry in the manner of Jean-Michel Frank.

In the comparatively compact dining room, which can be open or closed to the living room, I wanted to play with scale. A monumental Julian Schnabel canvas and an equally imposing Jean Perzel hanging fixture combine for drama. Below I set a Poul Kjærholm dining table—which, at twenty-six inches tall, is substantially lower than the standard—and matching chairs. Against the diminutive furniture, the Schnabel appears even more enormous, almost like an immersive installation. The success of this room and its exaggerated scales was a surprise to me, and it's become one of my favorite spaces.

A library adjacent to the dining room is paneled in oak to give it a moodier effect, much like the bed in the primary bedroom suite, which is inserted into a broad niche lined in suede panels. Throughout the home, the colors, materials, objects, and artworks we selected all reflect the singular spirit of my clients. While the apartment is not their primary residence, it is a dreamy and personal place for them to alight in New York, their second home.

PAGES 100–101   A Sean Scully painting is installed behind an Edward Wormley sofa for Dunbar in the living room. Other furnishings include Milo Baughman swivel chairs, Jacques Quinet cocktail tables, and Charlotte Perriand stools.

PAGES 102–3   The furniture ensemble in the less formal seating area of the living room encompasses an international roster of twentieth-century masters: a Harvey Probber sectional sofa, a Mathieu Matégot cocktail table, a Hans Wegner Papa Bear chair, a Jorge Zalszupin side table, and lighting by Jacques Adnet, Serge Mouille, and Luigi Caccia Dominioni.

PAGES 104–5   A Julian Schnabel painting has an outsize presence in the compact dining room, which is centered on a table and chairs by Poul Kjærholm set beneath a large Jean Perzel ceiling light. At one side of the space, a pair of sconces by Serge Mouille surmounts a Jacques Adnet sideboard.

PAGES 106–7   In the home office, a signature Horst P. Horst photograph of Cy Twombly hangs above a pair of rare Hans Wegner lounge chairs, while Arne Jacobsen side chairs pull up to an Edward Wormley partners desk.

PAGES 108–9   The bed is inserted into a broad niche lined in suede panels.

CONNECTICUT FARMHOUSE

Although the bones of this Connecticut country house date to the early 1700s, additions both historic and contemporary have enlarged the structure far beyond the scale typical of the period. A lofty nineteenth-century barn, for example, was attached to the main building in the 1930s. After living in the UK for several years, my young clients had returned to the United States with their new baby, intent on purchasing their first home. In all, the house encompasses 8,500 square feet, and since they arrived with only two pieces of furniture—a vintage trunk and a Danish desk—we had our work cut out for us.

The homeowners and I weren't interested in a slavish reproduction of a classic Colonial house. Instead, we wanted a more nuanced scheme that embraces American archetypes along with elements of Scandinavian design and contemporary pieces closer in age and sensibility to the clients' art collection. That spirit is perhaps best exemplified in the great room, which now occupies the former barn; this space set the tone for the rest of the house, in terms of both color and materials. The warm wood of the barrel vault was my starting point for a palette that includes rusty reds, pumpkin, and, reflecting the cool hues of the fieldstone fireplace, complementary silvery blues. Our principle for selecting furniture excluded anything too decorative; at its roots, the house is a simple farmhouse, and the pieces had to embody an honesty of form and be comfortable. The furnishings incorporate Arts and Crafts sofas and chairs by Paine, two vintage wingback chairs in red leather, and industrial elements such as a cast-iron coffee table that nods to the barn's utilitarian nature.

In the dining room, I surrounded a classic Stickley Mission dining table—the first piece my clients purchased for their new home—with a suite of chairs by French artist Pierre Abadie. The style collision of the traditional wood table and the sculptural folded-steel chairs creates a dialogue between the past and the present, sparking an aesthetic tension that lifts the project beyond a dry exercise in historical accuracy. Other modern additions—an Alvar Aalto chair in the entry, Hans Wegner wingback chairs in the library, Charlotte Perriand stools in the kitchen—generate a similar type of creative friction.

With the placement of the clients' art collection, which includes prominent works by Jack Pierson, Carroll Dunham, Gregory Crewdson, Elmgreen & Dragset, and Harland Miller, the duel between the modern and traditional kicks into overdrive.

PAGES 114–15   Arts and Crafts furnishings and other vernacular forms respond to the humble, utilitarian nature of the great room's architecture.

PAGE 116   Chairs by French artist Pierre Abadie pull up to a Gustav Stickley table in the dining room. The sconces are by Jules Wabbes.

PAGE 118   A Paul McCobb chair joins a Danish rosewood desk in the office.

PAGE 119   Hans Wegner Papa Bear chairs offer an ideal spot to enjoy the office fireplace.

PAGES 120–21   A Gregory Crewdson photograph overlooks the seating area of the primary bedroom.

PAGE 122   The primary bathroom is centered on a Gothic Revival table with an antique Dutch stool.

PAGE 123   In a guest room, early twentieth-century cog lights nod to the attenuated lines of the hammered steel bed frame.

PAGE 125   Charlotte Perriand stools pull up to the kitchen island.

HIGH LINE APARTMENT

This apartment for two men in the real estate business is in a new building designed by architect Thomas Juul-Hansen in New York City's Chelsea neighborhood. The structure straddles the High Line, the popular public park and greenway built on a historic elevated rail line. My design responds not only to the taut, modernist lines of Juul-Hansen's building but also to the colors and energy of the park below and the clean aesthetic of the homeowners.

The interior architecture and finishings are impeccable, with a distinctly masculine attitude—the kitchen is paneled entirely in charcoal-gray-stained wood, with the cabinet doors edged in a band of luminous polished brass—and it was easy for me to play off the character of the space. The generous living room is anchored by a thick, steel-blue mohair rug atop a larger flatweave carpet in a similar tone. The stacking effect helps delineate and focus the social space within the broader volume of the room, and imparts a plushness underfoot and to the overall atmosphere. Layered on top are a neatly tailored custom sofa and daybed, along with two Hans Wegner Papa Bear wingback chairs, a personal favorite, well loved for their sculptural grace and comfort. The color palette draws from the neutral-to-cool range of blues, grays, and taupes, with strategic accents like the red shade on a classic Arredoluce Triennale floor lamp.

Although the dining area is open to the living room, a newly installed partial wall shelters the media room without interrupting the flow of space. The rosewood Round dining chairs are another unimpeachable Wegner design. In the couple's bedroom, custom nightstands, made of highly figured wood encased in metal frames powder-coated in mustard yellow, coupled with a chunky bespoke lamp of black-and-gold marble, neatly sum up the apartment's vibe—crisp, strong, and quietly elegant.

PAGES 130–31   Hans Wegner wingback chairs, an Angelo Lelli Triennale lamp for Arredoluce,
                Fritz Hansen lounges, a custom sofa, and a Shawn Henderson Mercury daybed
                convene in the airy living room.

PAGE 133   A Judith Godwin painting hangs above a Kurt Østervig bar cabinet.

PAGES 134–35   The dining room is outfitted with Hans Wegner's classic Round chairs and
                artwork by Frank Wimberley.

PAGE 136   In a corner of the primary bedroom, a dresser by Edward Wormley for Dunbar is
                paired with a vintage Italian lounge chair and a Jasper Morrison side table.

HAMPTONS WATERFRONT RETREAT

In this newly built house in the chic Hamptons hamlet of Water Mill, the interiors accentuate and amplify the tailored lines and spruce modern spirit of the architectural shell crafted by Stelle Lomont Rouhani Architects, with whom I worked closely to select interior woods and finishes. The overall palette is decidedly neutral, deferring to the water views—of Jule Pond and the Atlantic—and verdant landscape that unfold through broad expanses of glass. In this arcadian retreat the interior appointments were calculated for sophistication as well as subtlety, not overt decorative bravado.

The living room, set within a soaring double-height volume, typifies our approach. Generously scaled custom sofas and lounge chairs set the tone for comfort and entertainment amid the beauty of nature. Marble side tables by Angelo Mangiarotti and three-arm Arredoluce standing lights with white shades add grace notes of classic European modernism to the ensemble without disrupting the tranquil palette. Vintage walnut side tables from Dunbar pick up the warmth of the slatted wood ceiling, and a custom chandelier by glass artist Jeremy Maxwell Wintrebert, with ethereal, organically shaped pendants that resemble drifting jellyfish or some other sea creature, underscores the serene character of the space.

The symphony of white and off-white hues extends into the open dining area, which is anchored by a fireplace elevation of highly textured ceramic panels by Peter Lane, a master of clay. In contrast to the lightness of the living, dining, and kitchen zones, the walls of the media room are upholstered in marine-blue linen, with curtains in the same fabric. Other splashes of blue appear in the upholstery of the Hans Wegner wingback chairs on one side of the living room and in the shimmering Moroccan tiles that sheathe a powder room on the main level. Despite these strategic hits of color, the home's overall palette remains quiet, providing a restrained backdrop for the clients' vibrant art collection.

PAGES 142–43   Two oil paintings by Enoc Perez and a sculpture by John Chamberlain add splashes of color to an otherwise monochromatic palette. The taut lines and clean forms of the upholstered seating harmonize with the crisp planes of the architecture. A custom chandelier by glass artist Jeremy Maxwell Wintrebert evokes the drifting forms of jellyfish.

PAGE 144   Stacking carpets one atop another helps to define and focus more intimate spaces. Here, at one side of the voluminous living room, a pair of Hans Wegner Papa Bear chairs is joined by a vintage concrete-top cocktail table by Dutch sculptor and mosaic artist Paul Kingma.

PAGE 145   In contrast to the bright white palette of the living room, the media room is sheathed in marine-blue linen, with curtains in the same fabric. The swivel chairs are by Edward Wormley, and the table lamp is a classic Max Ingrand design.

PAGE 146   The dining area is anchored by a fireplace elevation of ceramic tiles by artist Peter Lane.

PAGE 147   Digital art by Julian Opie hangs in the stairwell.

PAGE 148   A mirror by Sam Orlando Miller adds a bit of color and sparkle to the tranquil primary bedroom. The teardrop chairs are by Milo Baughman.

PAGE 150   An artwork by Francisco Valverde adorns the bedroom.

MY HILLSDALE HOME

This 1830 Eyebrow Colonial in Hillsdale, New York, is my own country house, a place that reflects my personal tastes, my sensibility as a designer, and also a bit of nostalgia for summers spent at my family's camp in the Adirondacks. It's a laid-back, grown-up version of a cherished childhood hangout. Over the fifteen years I've had the place, it's helped me figure out for myself how a home should truly function. It has been a fruitful and inspiring design laboratory, a space to test ideas and work more organically than I'm able to on a client project. Filled with things that I've collected over many years, it often surprises me to see how the rooms fall into place, coming together in unexpected compositions. The decor represents a fusion of classic Americana with the humble beauty of Swedish country homes, both of which rely on spare yet studied arrangements of objects and art to nurture a mood of easy repose.

I've done three renovations to the house. The last one followed a fire that destroyed a 1970 addition, and I took the opportunity to add a thousand square feet that include a new master suite and a commodious kitchen. (Over the years, I've realized how much I enjoy cooking and hosting, so a large, inviting kitchen was essential.) Architectural details of the historic house—rough-hewn beams, original wood floors, and Craftsman-like wall paneling—were either preserved or recreated in places where they'd been stripped away. While the modern additions—including the new screened porch and primary bedroom suite above—are clearly distinguishable from the original structure, they were designed to be sympathetic in materials, texture, and spirit.

The living room epitomizes the American-Scandinavian interface in the juxtaposition of an American wingback chair with furnishings by Kaare Klint, Frits Henningsen, and Kerstin Hörlin-Holmquist. The great room, wrapped in panels of white-painted pine, is the perfect scale for entertaining my family and friends. Here, the overall white palette is accented with blue and gold, and the decor follows the theme of the living room—vintage pieces of Swedish, French, and Danish origin are set alongside companionable American designs and custom pieces. The bedrooms are designed, as bedrooms should be, for peace, quiet, and rest. I placed a bathtub in a sunny corner of my bedroom, where I can soak and take in the view of the pond and treetops.

I love being in the thick of New York City from my apartment in Manhattan, but my place upstate—surrounded by things I love, close to where I grew up, and with family nearby—is where I feel really at home.

PAGE 152   A sofa by Kaare Klint, side chair by Kerstin Hörlin-Holmquist, and table by Frits Henningsen demonstrate my passion for Scandinavian design. The drawing above the fireplace is by Louise Bonnet.

PAGES 154–55   Vintage American and European pieces mingle amicably in the living room, all united by their unpretentious forms, neutral palette, and fine craftsmanship. The painting is by Genieve Figgis.

PAGE 156   A Maureen Fullam mirror is installed above a cabinet by the Danish workshop Rud. Rasmussen.

PAGE 157   A Barber Osgerby pendant light hangs above a Chris Lehrecke table in the dining area. The multipaneled photograph is by David Hilliard.

PAGES 158–59   I set up the great room for easy, comfortable entertaining, with lots of seating options, including a pair of Guillerme et Chambron lounge chairs and two vintage Art Deco armchairs.

PAGES 160–61   Although the kitchen is a modern addition, the brick floor and lime plaster wall finish make sympathetic overtures to the original historic structure.

PAGES 162–63   I placed a bathtub in a sunny corner of my bedroom so I could take a relaxing soak with a view from the comfort of my private refuge. The watercolor is by my nephew, Finn Johnsson, and the photograph is by Michael Stuetz.

ASPEN RANCH

For this ground-up mountain house in Aspen, my goal was to orchestrate harmony between the interiors and the lean, linear forms devised by my collaborator, Robbins Architecture. My selection of interior finishes and furnishings honors the angular minimalism of the architecture while gently adding notes of warmth as a counterbalance to the concrete structure. Since the house sits on roughly eighty acres, with stunning views of Aspen and the Rocky Mountains, there was no need for ostentatious or dramatic gestures. The wow moments were already there.

Immediately upon entry, a wall paneled in dark, rich wood provides a contrast to the light oak floors and stairs of the entry hall, as well as the expanses of glass that connect the interior with the surrounding landscape. Another wall of wood anchors the living/dining room sweep on the upper level. Per my clients' request, I used vintage furnishings mostly as accents. The majority of the furniture includes clean-lined custom pieces and contemporary creations that speak the same design language as the architecture. A chunky oatmeal-colored wool rug sits atop a broad flatweave to suggest a subtle boundary between the living and dining zones. Throw pillows in oxblood red play up the intentionally soft, neutral palette of whites, grays, and browns.

In the kitchen, where sliding pocket walls of glass open onto an outdoor deck and the pool beyond, I installed a long, low banquette for the homeowners' grown children, who are frequent visitors, to work or relax while their parents do the cooking. A sleek tubular pendant light hangs above an island with seating for six, further encouraging social interaction in the kitchen. Here, as throughout the house, the space is designed with restraint and comfort in mind—all the better to appreciate the glory of the mountain landscape.

PAGE 170   In the dining room, Hans Brattrud chairs pull up to a custom table beneath an
            Apparatus Cloud chandelier.

PAGE 173   A Joel Shapiro sculpture is installed in the entry.

PAGES 174–75 Custom sofas, a shearling-wrapped bench, and a pair of Luca Nichetto armchairs
              surround a broad cocktail table in the living room. The painting is by Bo Joseph.

PAGES 176–77 BDDW counter stools and a generous banquette support the kitchen's role as a
              lively social space.

PAGE 178   A Christophe Gaignon mirror sculpture surmounts a modern desk in the office.

PAGE 179   The soothing, monochromatic palette of the primary bedroom is attuned to the
            color of the wood paneling. The artwork is by Yayoi Kusama.

FRENCH QUARTER TOWN HOUSE

Since its completion, this grand nineteenth-century Creole town house in the French Quarter of New Orleans has been considered one of the most splendid homes in the Vieux Carré. For this special residence, I wanted to create an environment that not only exalts the house's brilliant historical features but also reflects the distinctive personalities of the homeowners and the vivid, eccentric spirit of the city. Channeling the fertile, cross-cultural history of the Big Easy, but leaning into French design, I selected a mélange of furnishings that spans vintage twentieth-century treasures by André Sornay, Serge Roche, and Maison Jansen, heavily carved mirrors and cabinets from the previous century, and signature chairs and tables by avant-garde contemporary masters Mattia Bonetti and the brothers Simon and Nikolai Haas.

Given the expansive scale of the project—the house is nearly nine thousand square feet, with lofty thirteen-foot ceilings—the decorative moves needed to be bold. In the main parlor, which measures twenty-five feet square, I paired a custom Jansen-inspired sofa with four large Bonetti lounge chairs beneath an existing crystal chandelier that harks back to an earlier era of New Orleans glamour. Artworks by Evan Holloway and Angel Otero ground the composition in the present and play off an imposing antique carved-wood cabinet that is a family heirloom. In the similarly scaled dining room, where French doors open onto a gallery, the mahogany-topped dining table and reproduction Louis XVI chairs in black leather occupy one side of the space, balanced by a curvaceous corner banquette and custom swivel chairs for informal socializing on the opposite side.

As a testament to the scale of the residence, the lighting fixture that crowns the primary bedroom is fully four feet square. For a splash of New Orleans luxe, the custom four-poster bed is wrapped in blue velvet, and windowed doors leading to the second-floor gallery are treated to draperies in the same fabric. An antique Italian daybed in the corner is covered in a similarly hued mohair. A Scandinavian lounge chair and ottoman are upholstered in shearling for chromatic and textural contrast, and the whole composition is set on a sprawling jute carpet dyed a greenish blue. Another estimable collection of contemporary art further energizes a house designed to skip to the beat of a city where the party never ends.

PAGE 184   Club chairs by André Sornay bracket a Maison Jansen cocktail table in the office. The painting is by Kristy Luck.

PAGE 185   A vintage Art Deco desk holds a corner of the office.

PAGES 186–87   An Evan Holloway sculpture makes a dramatic counterpoint to an antique crystal chandelier in the living room, where Garouste and Bonetti chairs surround a Haas Brothers book stand converted into a cocktail table. The painting at left is by Angel Otero.

PAGES 188–89   An Elmgreen & Dragset sculpture mediates the two halves of the capacious dining room. One side of the space has Louis XVI–style chairs set around a table of that period, while the less formal side of the room features custom tufted banquettes with barrel chairs in the style of Edward Wormley. The paintings are by Georgina Gratrix, left, and Tom Keyes, and the console is by Serge Roche.

PAGE 190   A wall sculpture by Brie Ruais anchors a corner of the dining room.

PAGE 192   A Cesare Lacca settee sits at the foot of a four-poster bed wrapped in blue velvet. The custom plaster pendant light measures four feet square. The painting is by Genieve Figgis.

PAGE 193   An antique daybed of figured elm holds a corner of the primary bedroom.

PAGE 194   Paintings by Neil Stokoe, right, and Jerry Zeniuk flank the fireplace in a sitting room off the primary bedroom.

PAGE 195   A mirrored and gilded bed reflects the pink palette of a guest room.

UTAH MOUNTAIN HOUSE

This bright, airy ski house and family getaway in Park City, Utah, should put to rest the old canard that modern design is cold or sterile. Although the furnishings are clean and tailored, and the palette overwhelmingly neutral, with well-deployed shots of blues and purples, this is a place of warmth and comfort, eminently hospitable for my clients. A design-savvy Hong Kong–based couple with two young sons, they wanted a space that was light in spirit and full of character, with a customized point of view. The decor encompasses signature pieces by masters of design from the past and current centuries, but nothing comes across as trendy or conspicuously avant-garde. Instead, the house provides a meticulously groomed yet almost playful backdrop for family life.

The living room exemplifies the ambience of elevated warmth. The diagonal lines of a deep sectional sofa provide a counterpoint to the organic forms of the trees and mountains that cradle the house. For a bit of textural and chromatic contrast, the white sofa and pale plaster walls are juxtaposed with a fireplace surround of dark metal with a soft, patinated finish. Midcentury chairs covered in emerald-green velvet introduce a flash of color, and an unapologetic note of drama comes in the form of a dazzling Vincenzo De Cotiis cocktail table with a highly figured top of marble and Murano glass set on a base of silvered brass—a small masterpiece that invites close inspection.

Other special pieces and decorative flourishes pepper the laid-back ensembles of furniture throughout the home. In the dining area, barrel-back chairs surround a Damien Gernay table beneath a sculptural custom pendant light in glowing polished brass. A serpentine banquette, with deep green fabric, offers a cozy seating area at the base of the stairs on the lowest level, a perfect place for a young family of four to work on a puzzle and unwind after a day on the slopes.

PAGE 198 — A sculptural mirror by Christian Astuguevieille highlights the entry.

PAGES 200–201 — Among the treasures in the living room are a Vincenzo De Cotiis cocktail table of marble and Murano glass, a Campana Brothers cork armchair, a stained glass lamp by Maarten De Ceulaer, and a vintage rope floor lamp by Adrien Audoux and Frida Minet. Above the mantel is a glass mosaic by Shahzia Sikander.

PAGE 202 — Ruemmler chairs surround a Damien Gernay table beneath a custom chandelier in the dining room.

PAGE 203 — A cozy lounge is outfitted with de Sede chairs, a chunky Martin Massé cocktail table, and a classic Poul Henningsen pendant light.

PAGE 204 — In the study, a vintage Paavo Tynell chandelier crowns a custom desk with a Pierre Jeanneret chair. Artwork by Thiago Rocha Pitta.

PAGE 205 — An encaustic painting by Martin Kline hangs above a table by Odd Matter.

PAGES 206–7 — The primary bedroom features a Maren Kloppmann porcelain wall sculpture, a Campana Brothers chandelier, Romeo Sozzi bedside tables, vintage Otto Schultz lounge chairs, and a clay table by Decio Studio.

PAGE 208 — Jean Royère stools pull up to a richly hued marble bar in the game room.

PAGE 209 — An Angelo Mangiarotti table is cradled in a serpentine banquette at the base of a staircase. Artwork by Douglas Melini.

PAGES 210–11 — The game room has Paolo Buffa chairs, a cocktail table by J.M. Szymanski, and a Nir Meiri chandelier suspended above a James Perse ping-pong table.

PAGE 213 — A vintage Angelo Mangiarotti table sits beside a Jan Ekselius lounge chair in a bedroom. Behind is a cabinet by Piet Hein Eek.

Just north of Natchez, Mississippi, Wyolah, a country estate constructed in 1836 for an Irish doctor, sprawls over one hundred acres, with a three-story Greek Revival house and eight outbuildings. When my client, a writer, director, and old friend, asked me if I would consider working on a house like this, a building listed on the National Register of Historic Places, I jumped at the chance. For this natural storyteller and host with an open-door policy, a home with color and personality that was both hospitable and compelling was essential. The project proved to be a feat of revitalization. Working with restoration consultant Thomas E. Goodman, my mission was to resurrect the property in a manner that pays homage to the best of its antebellum roots while ushering it into the here and now, both aesthetically and functionally.

Over three years, parts of the main house and many of the outlying structures were reimagined to create spaces more in tune with contemporary usage, while adhering to the National Register's rigorous rules. The house's third floor, formerly a raw attic, was converted into four bedrooms with baths en suite and a small kitchen and laundry room. One outbuilding, the erstwhile kitchen, was transformed into a one-bedroom guesthouse, as was the charming columned office built by Wyolah's first owner. The old commissary, connected to the main house by a newly constructed breezeway, is now the primary kitchen.

The house's faux-marble mantels and faux-grain doors, which had all been painted over, were meticulously restored. The dining room walls now sport a romantic mural of local flora and fauna by Mississippi artist Don Jacobs. The center of Wyolah's action is the elegantly proportioned music room, where the homeowner's friends gather and play. The room's decor, taking its cues from a velvet-covered borne, typifies the new aesthetic sensibility, in which period antiques and archetypal totems of Southern hospitality are recontextualized in time-spanning ensembles that incorporate vintage midcentury furnishings of far-flung pedigree and contemporary custom designs. That same energy extends into the bedrooms, where classic nineteenth-century four-posters and other period beds are juxtaposed with midcentury lighting and sprightly wall coverings.

Wyolah today is a place that celebrates the comforts of home, the joy of friends and family, and the promise of the present—a place that evokes and rewards curiosity and creativity.

PAGE 218   A William-and-Mary-style settee and an ebonized Biedermeier cabinet grace the entry hall.

PAGE 219   The parlor is outfitted with an ensemble of nineteenth-century furnishings, including a French campaign daybed, an Italian wingback chair, and an English crystal-and-bronze chandelier.

PAGES 220–21   Crowned by a nineteenth-century crystal chandelier, the music room features a pair of midcentury Italian wingback chairs and a custom velvet-covered borne.

PAGES 222–23   Artist Don Jacobs wrapped the dining room in a mural that pays homage to the Mississippi landscape. The custom dining table was fabricated from the wood of a pecan tree on the property.

PAGES 224–25   Glazed brick tiles set the mood in the kitchen. The vintage lounge chair is by Swedish designer Carl Malmsten.

PAGES 228–29   A nineteenth-century neoclassical canopy bed anchors the primary bedroom.

PAGES 232–33   The walls of the sitting room off the primary bedroom are sheathed in a recycled embroidered tarp from JRJ Tecidos.

ACKNOWLEDGMENTS

First and foremost, profound thanks to all my clients. Without your trust and support, this book would not have been possible.

Thank you to the team at Monacelli and Phaidon: Keith Fox, Philip Ruppel, William Norwich, and Jenny Florence. To Phil Kovacevich for his beautiful design, and to Mayer Rus for his eloquent words. A special thank-you to Stephen Kent Johnson for capturing my work with so much artistry and grace.

To Birch Coffey for his guidance over these years, and to Thad Hayes for helping me find my voice as a designer.

Thank you to everyone at my studio, past and present: Trisha Elliott, Jon Hindman, Pamela Mah, Mike Rupp, Lauren Slocumbe, Abby Driscoll, Andrew Vichosky, Derrick Sibley, Jim Fairfax, Gloria Morell, and, finally, Rachel Stearns, my studio director, who has been with me since the beginning.

To the talented artisans and vendors I've collaborated with over the years: thank you. Your contributions have been invaluable.

To all the editors who have championed my work: Margaret Russell, Robert Rufino, Whitney Robinson, Clinton Smith, Carolyn Englefield, Dan Rubinstein, Jacqueline Terrebonne, and Anthony Iannacci.

Finally, I am forever grateful to my dear friends and family for all their love, kindness, and encouragement.

CREDITS

MY WEST VILLAGE APARTMENT

New York, NY
800 square feet
General Contractor: Riverside Builders
Millworker: SFA Interiors

ASPEN MODERN RETREAT

Aspen, CO
9,000 square feet
Architect: Studio B Architecture + Interiors

GREENWICH VILLAGE TOWN HOUSE

New York, NY
5,500 square feet
Architect: Peter Pennoyer Architects
Landscape Architect: Madison Cox

WEST VILLAGE RESIDENCE

New York, NY
3,500 square feet
General Contractor: SilverLining Inc.

MONTANA CHALET

Big Sky, MT
15,000 square feet
Architect: Pearson Design Group
General Contractor: Highline Partners
Lightning Specialist: Sean O'Connor Lighting

RIVER-VIEW APARTMENT

New York, NY
3,200 square feet
General Contractor: Riverside Builders

CONNECTICUT FARMHOUSE

Lakeville, CT
8,500 square feet
General Contractor: Robert J. Campbell Jr. & Sons

HIGH LINE APARTMENT

New York, NY
2,100 square feet
General Contractor: Riverside Builders

HAMPTONS WATERFRONT RETREAT

Water Mill, NY
5,400 square feet
Architect: Stelle Lomont Rouhani Architects
Landscape Architect: LaGuardia Design Group

MY HILLSDALE HOME

Hillsdale, NY
3,200 square feet
Architect: Historical Concepts
General Contractor: Bart DeRocha

ASPEN RANCH

Aspen, CO
7,800 square feet
Architect: Robbins Architecture
Landscape Architect: Hoerr Schaudt
General Contractor: Harriman Construction Inc.
Lighting Specialist: Gregg Mackell, IALD

FRENCH QUARTER TOWN HOUSE

New Orleans, LA
8,350 square feet

UTAH MOUNTAIN HOUSE

Park City, UT
8,450 square feet
General Contractor: Magleby Construction

MISSISSIPPI COUNTRY ESTATE

Natchez, MS
12,000 square feet
Architect: Thomas E. Goodman
Landscape Architect: Damian Augsberger
General Contractor: Tony DeAngelis

SHAWN HENDERSON has been a fixture on the international design scene
for more than two decades. His work is synonymous with unpretentious luxury,
sophistication, and beauty. From his studio in New York City, he has spearheaded an
astonishing variety of residential and hospitality projects, each one uniquely responsive
to the exigencies of site, context, and the individual spirit of his clients. His interiors
privilege connoisseurship as well as comfort, drawing inspiration from the past to conjure
environments firmly rooted in the present, deftly attuned to the rituals of contemporary
life. Among his many accolades, Henderson has been named to *Architectural Digest*'s
prestigious AD100 and the Elle Decor A-List.

Library of Congress Control Number: 2021938439

ISBN 978-1-58093-583-8

Design by Phil Kovacevich

Printed in China

Monacelli
A Phaidon Company
65 Bleecker Street
New York, NY 10012
www.monacellipress.com